Designs and Doodles

By

Nanita Mayo Williams

Copyright @ 2020 Navita Mago Williams
All rights reserved.

No part of this book can be recreated or sold in any form without the Author's prior written permission.
Colored versions of the art may be shared with proper attribution.

ISBN: 9798567041284

This book belongs to

_____

Dear Buyer,

Congratulations on your purchase. This coloring book is not just a collection of designs. You will see that each page was made with thought and care to ensure a fun coloring experience. You can get as creative as you like and maybe even add something of your own as they do have space for you to doodle along!

Included in this book is also a general art section with pages that will give you a break from just designs and patterns.

The last two pages are comprised of "Thank you" in different languages. I was inspired from a kind lady in the the coffee shop, here in Berlin one fine morning, when I asked her if she spoke English, she responded casually, "yes I speak 4 languages!". So how many languages do you know?

You can use crayons, pastels, coloring pencils, pens, watercolors, markers or any other colors. I have only one suggestion, please slip a spare paper under the coloring sheets if you are using heavy markers, pens, water colors and such.

I hope you enjoy coloring these pages as much as I enjoyed making them. I would love to see your colored versions. You can share them with me many ways. All the social media details are on the 'about the author page'.

Happy coloring!

Best wishes always!

This book is dedicated to my Husband and my babies. They are a source of constant strength and I am able to do what I love, with their support and hugs.

Navila

About the Author

Navita is the founder of the art and illustration brand MINTY DESIGNS. She has been making art on paper, canvas, glass and ceramics for over 10 years.

Investment banker turned artist, she has had many experiences but her true heart is in colors and creating art.

She is now successfully designing home decor and print on demand merchandise.

Making coloring books is one of her many passions. She feels coloring books are a way to share her creativity and co-create with all coloring enthusiasts.

Navita Mago Williams

Email: contact@mintydesigns.net
Instagram- @navita.loves.colors
Facebook- www.facebook.com/MintyArts/

Contents

1. Floral
2. Fish
3. Birds
4. Only flowers
5. Dotty pattern 1
6. Waves
7. Fruit and veg
8. Cake
9. Hearts
10. Patterned pattern
11. Knitted wallhanging
12. Angel wings
13. Fish fins
14. Dark ink 1
15. Dark ink 2
16. Floral sun
17. Dotty pattern 2
18. Bees mosaic
19. Bird garden
20. Bird garden with pots
21. Cycle in the yard
22. Small Country town
23. Home by the river
24. Country side mash
25. Block art
26. Tattoo art
27. Dogs
28. Cats
29. Thank you- English , French , German Spanish
30. Thank you - Chinese , Japanese , Hindi

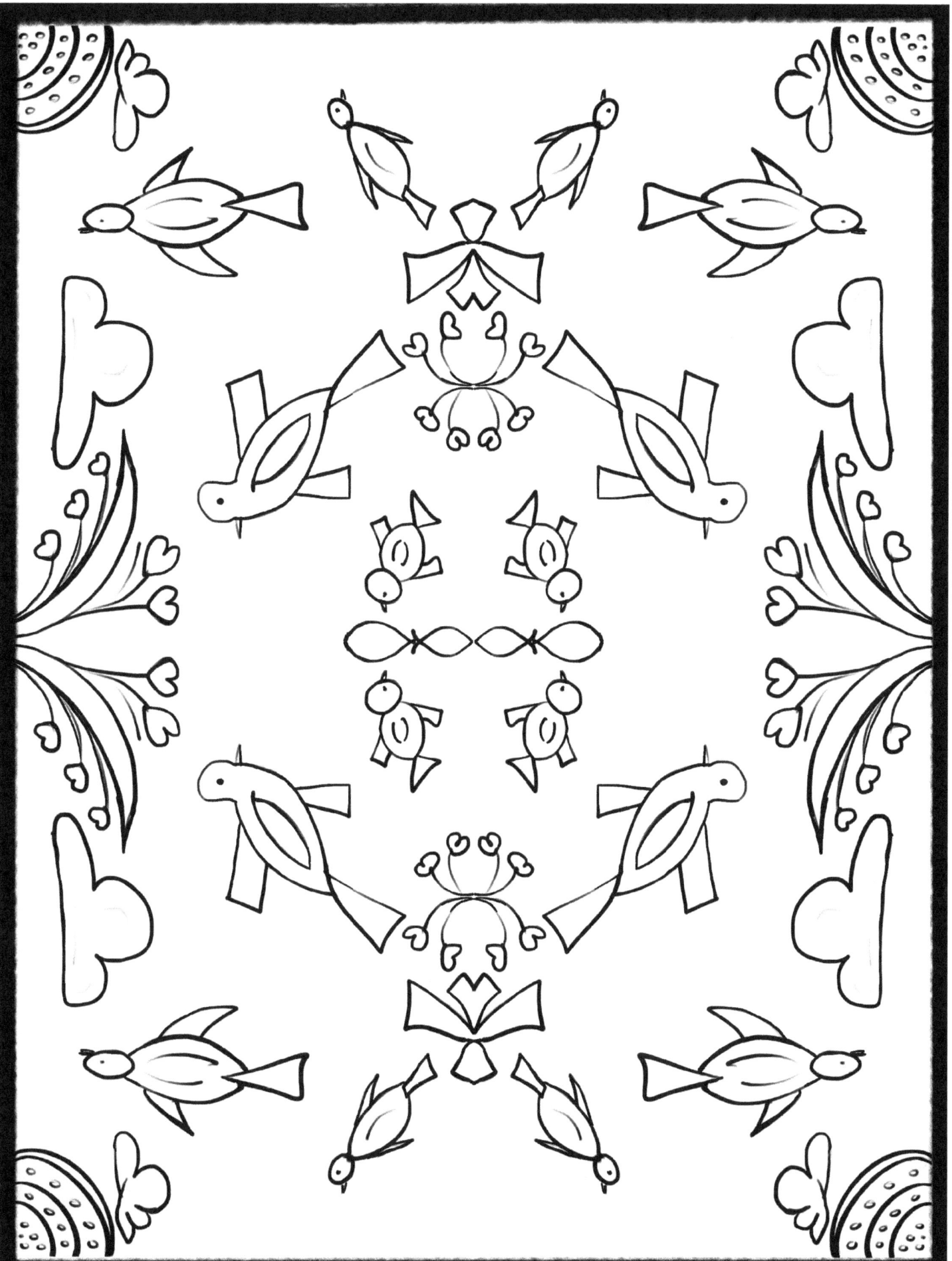

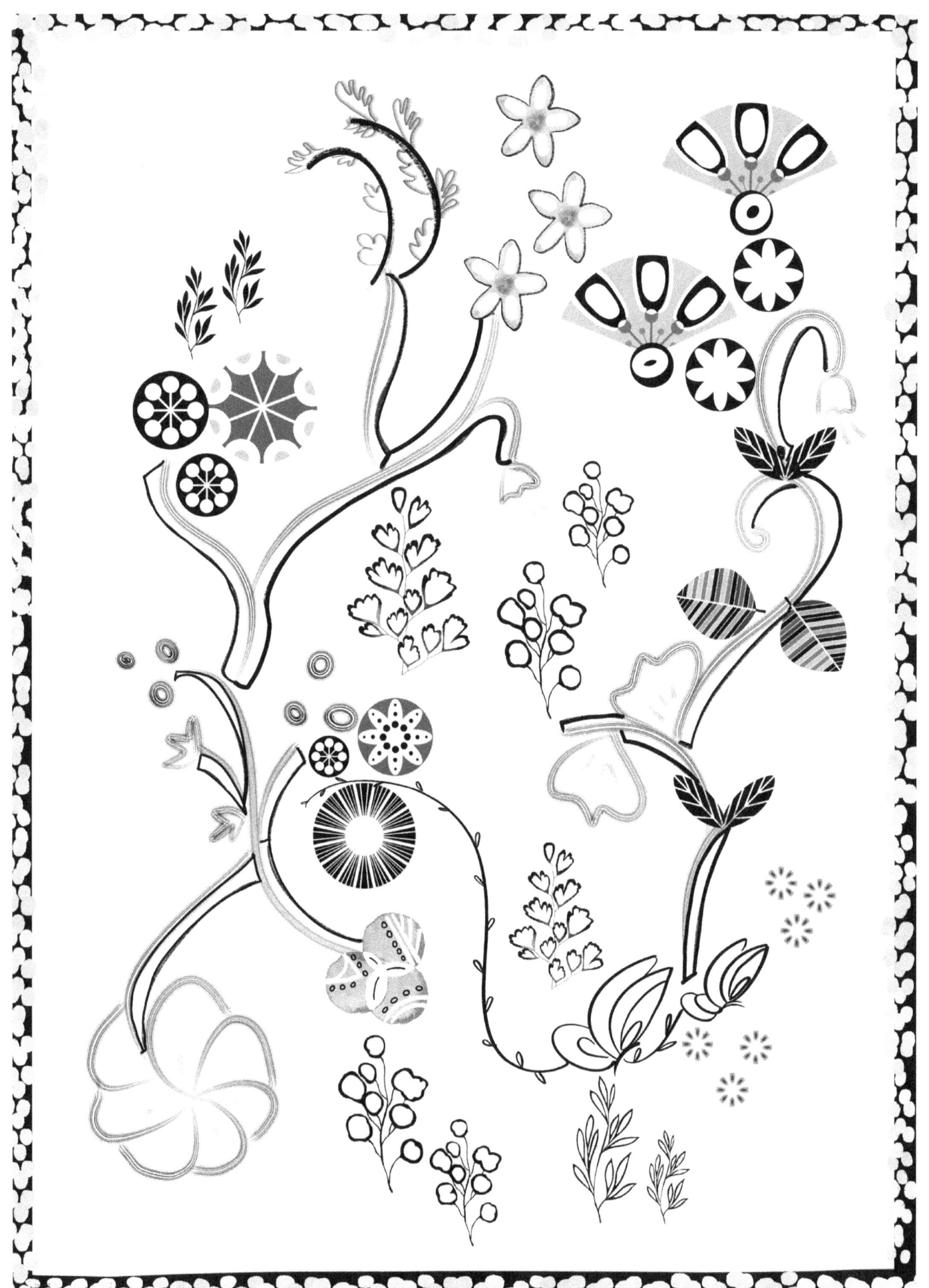

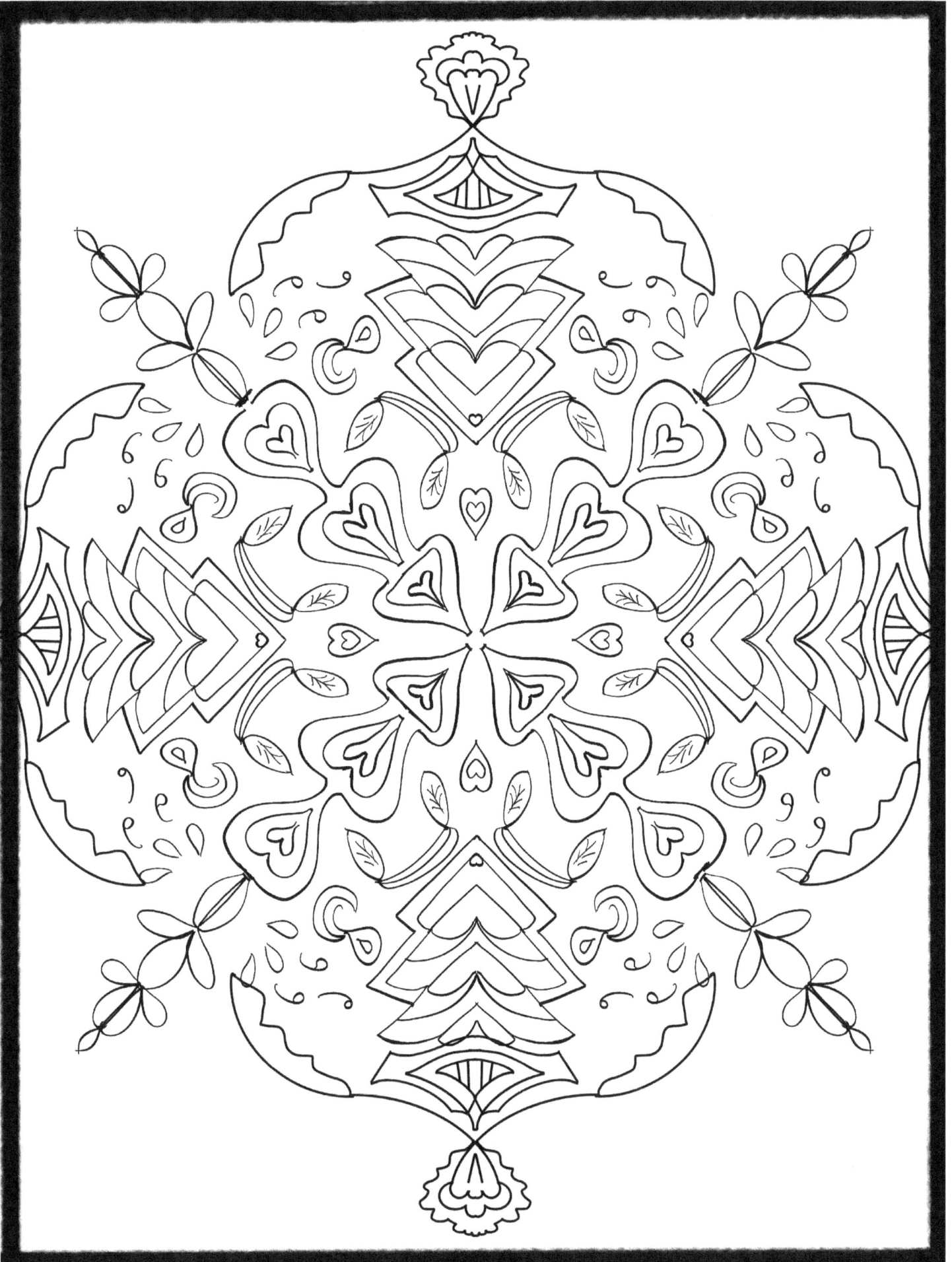

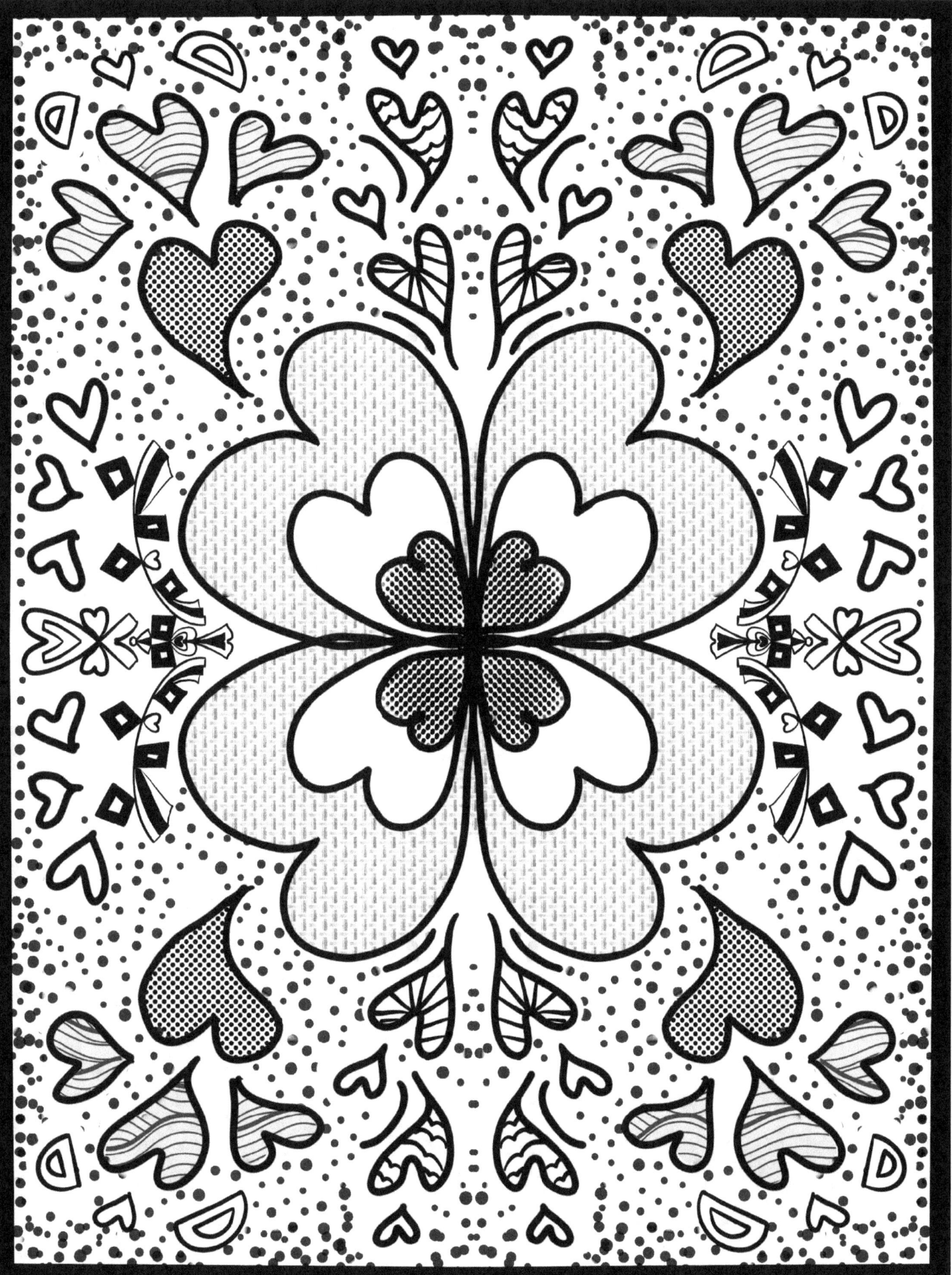

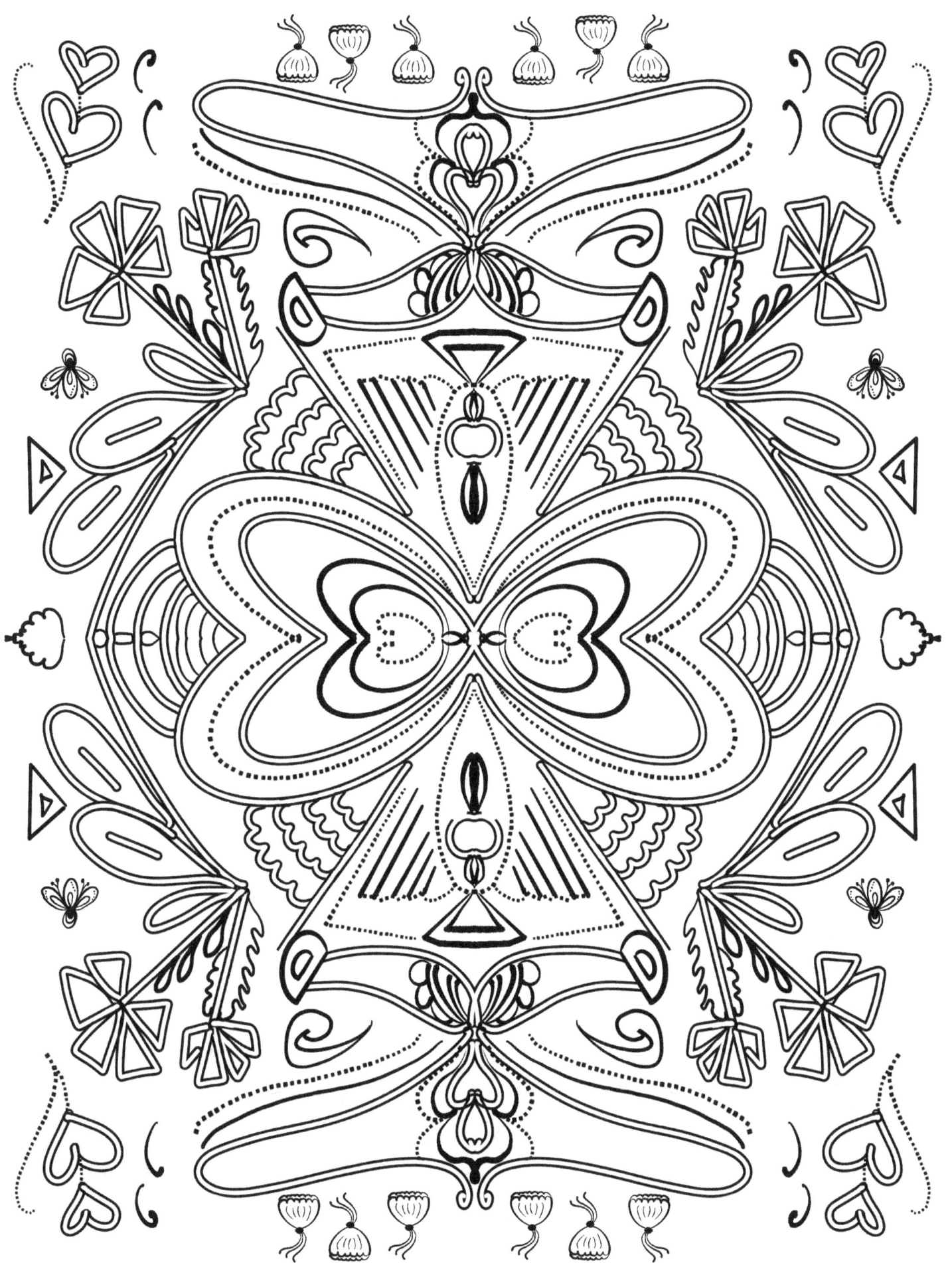

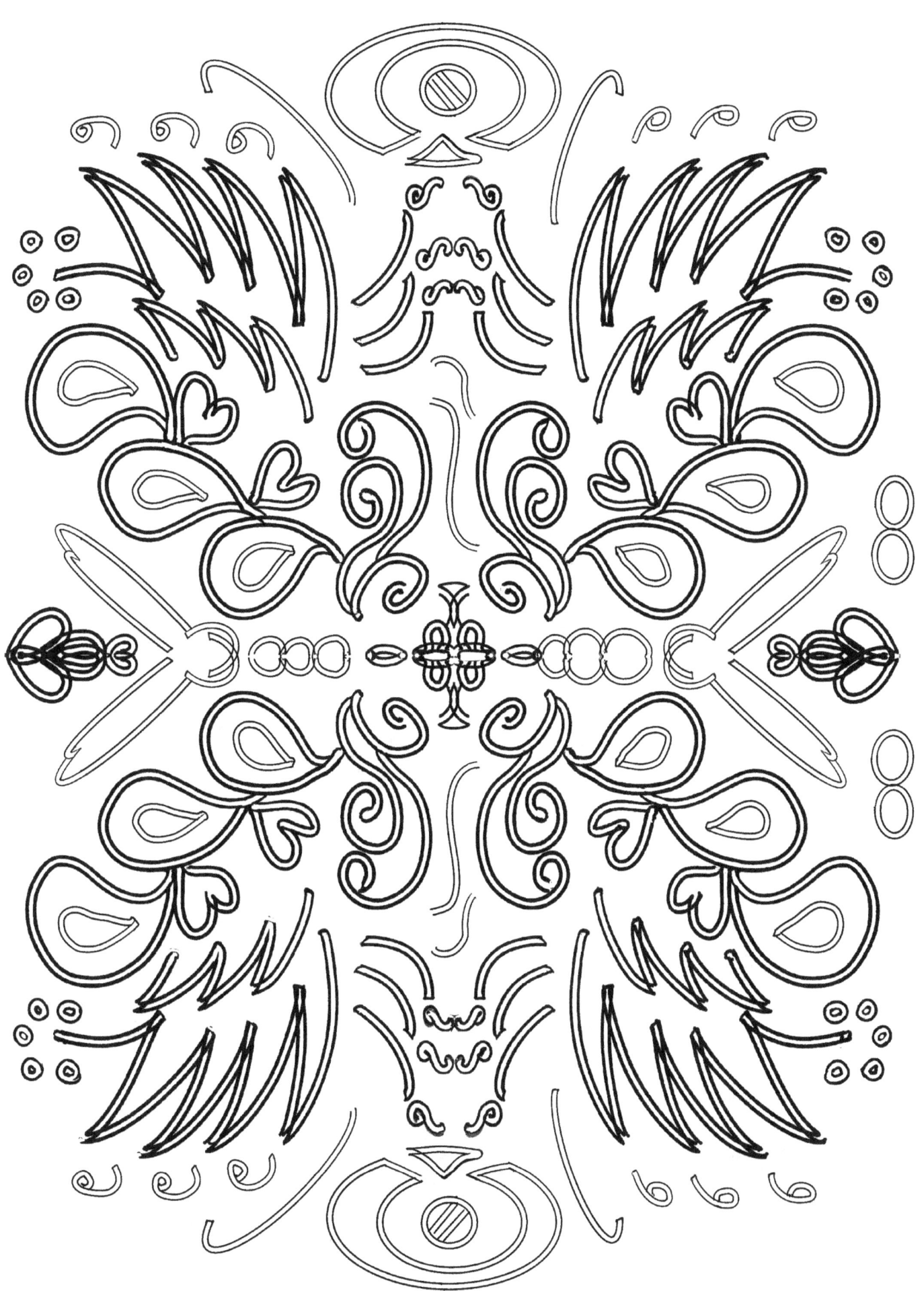

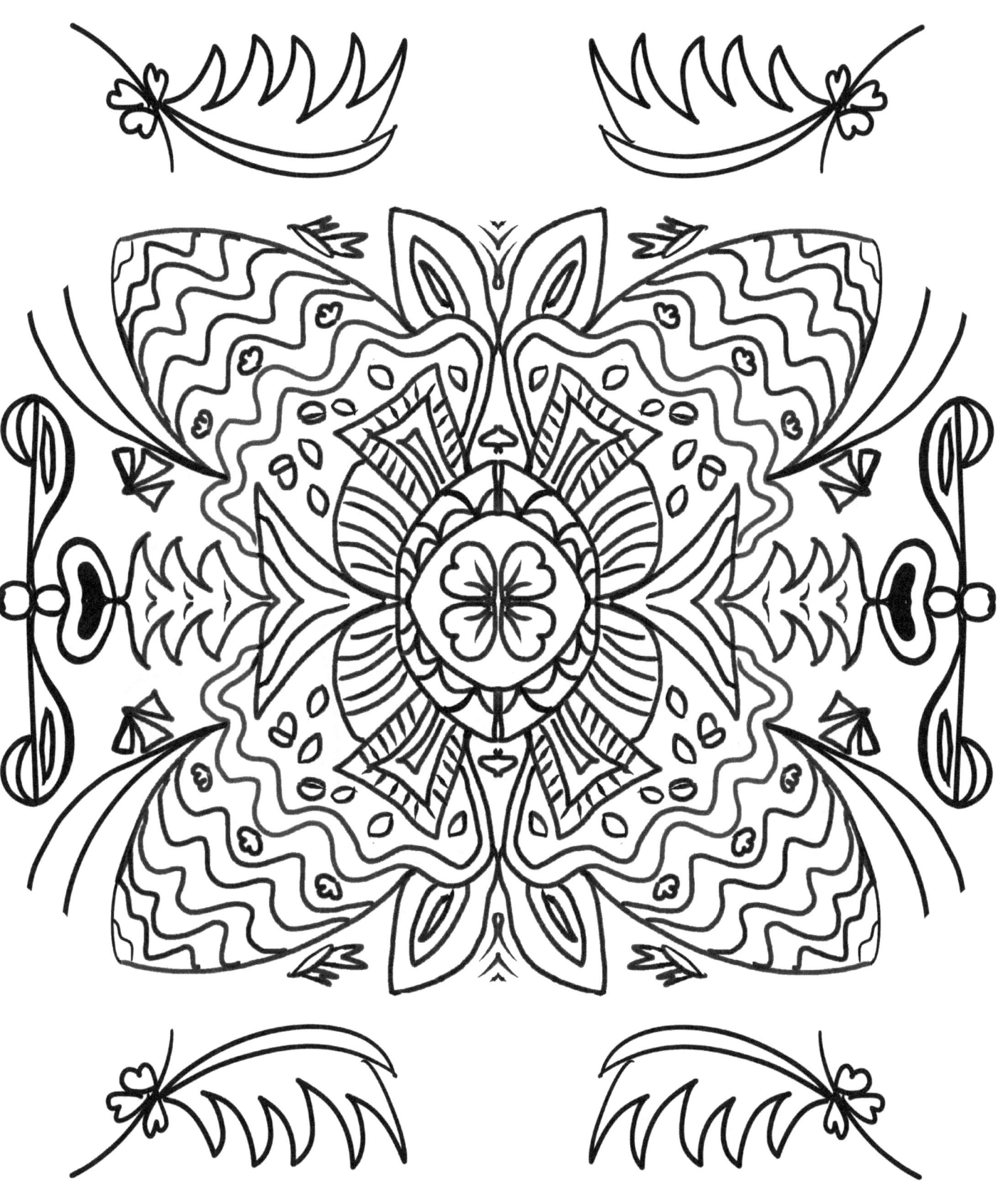

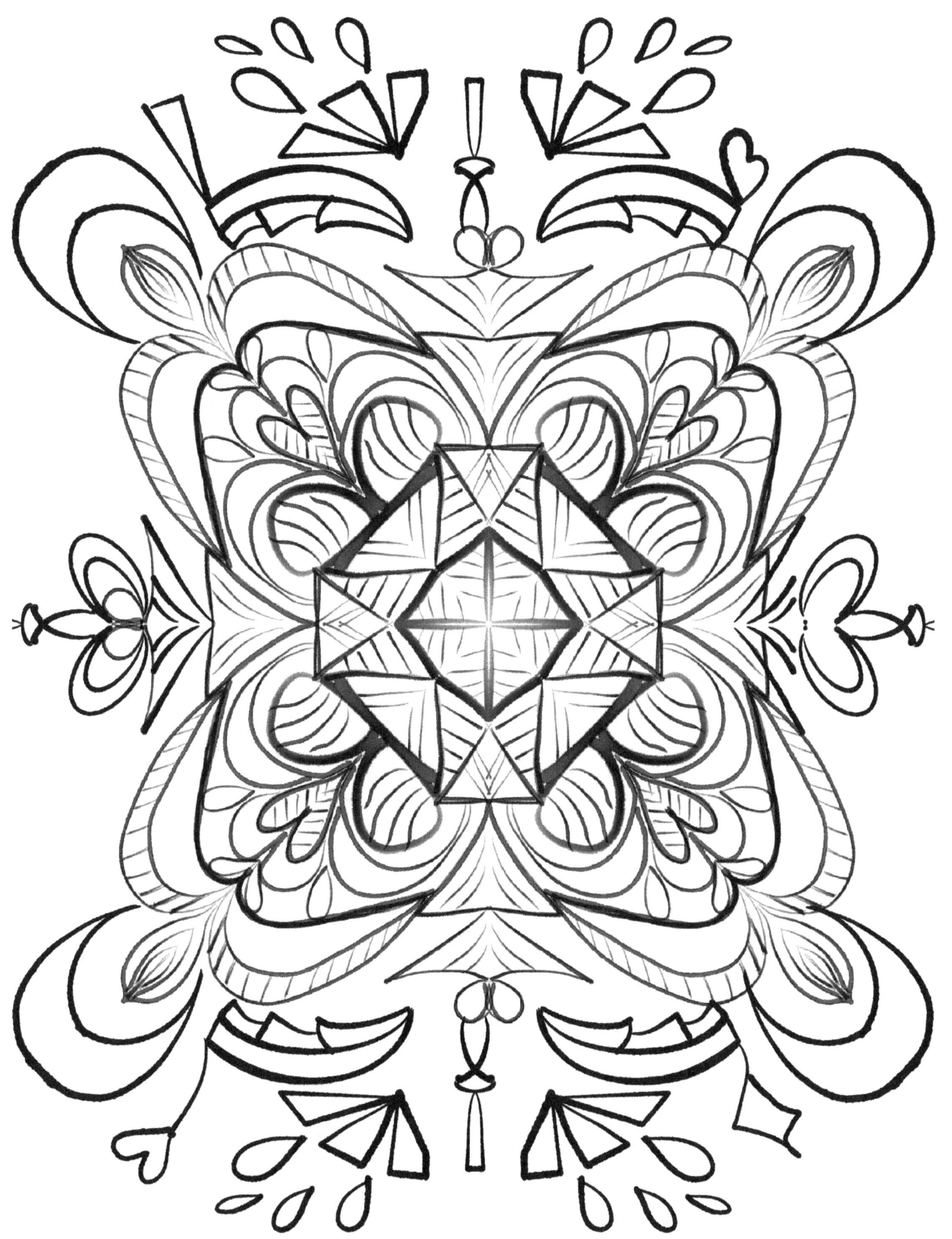

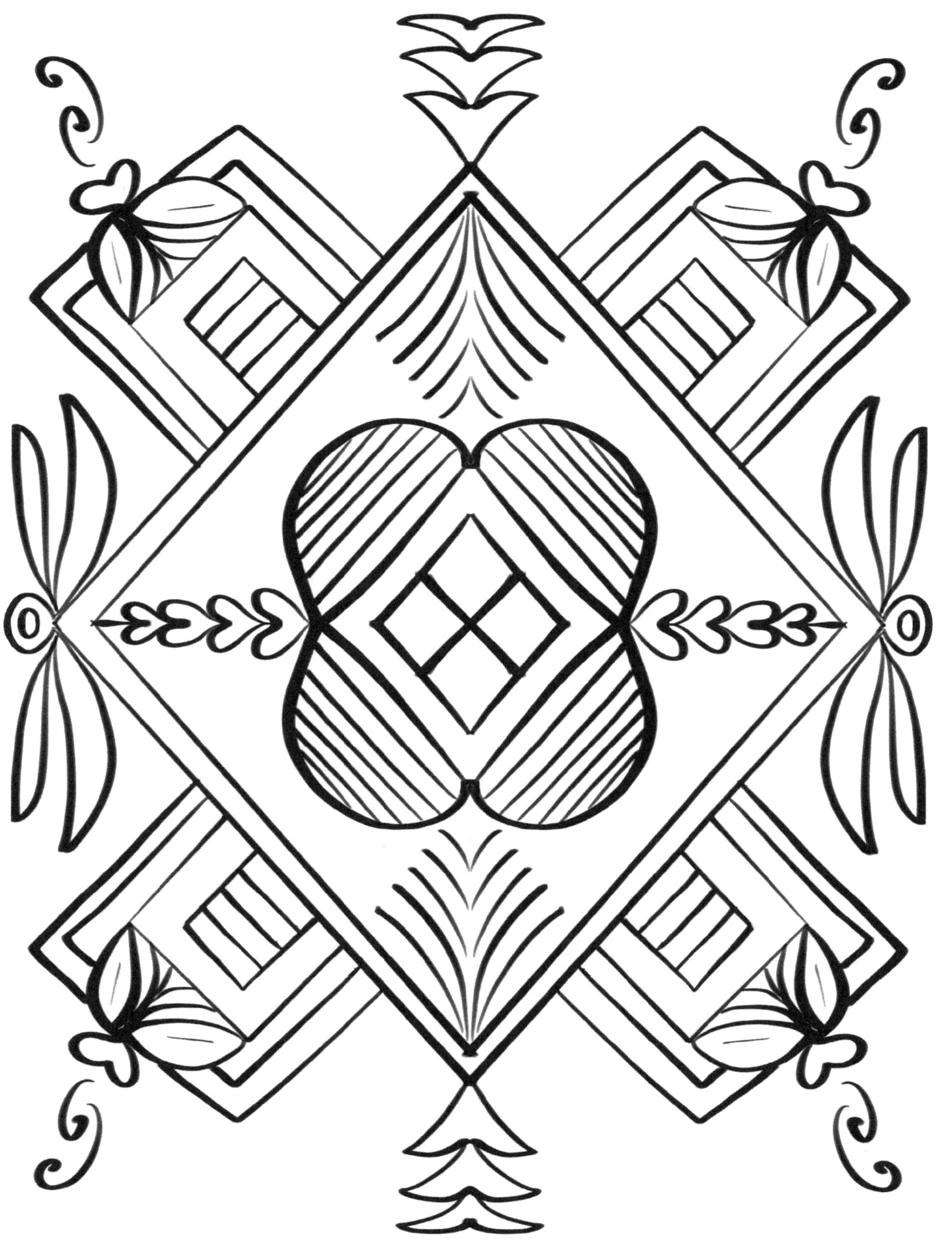

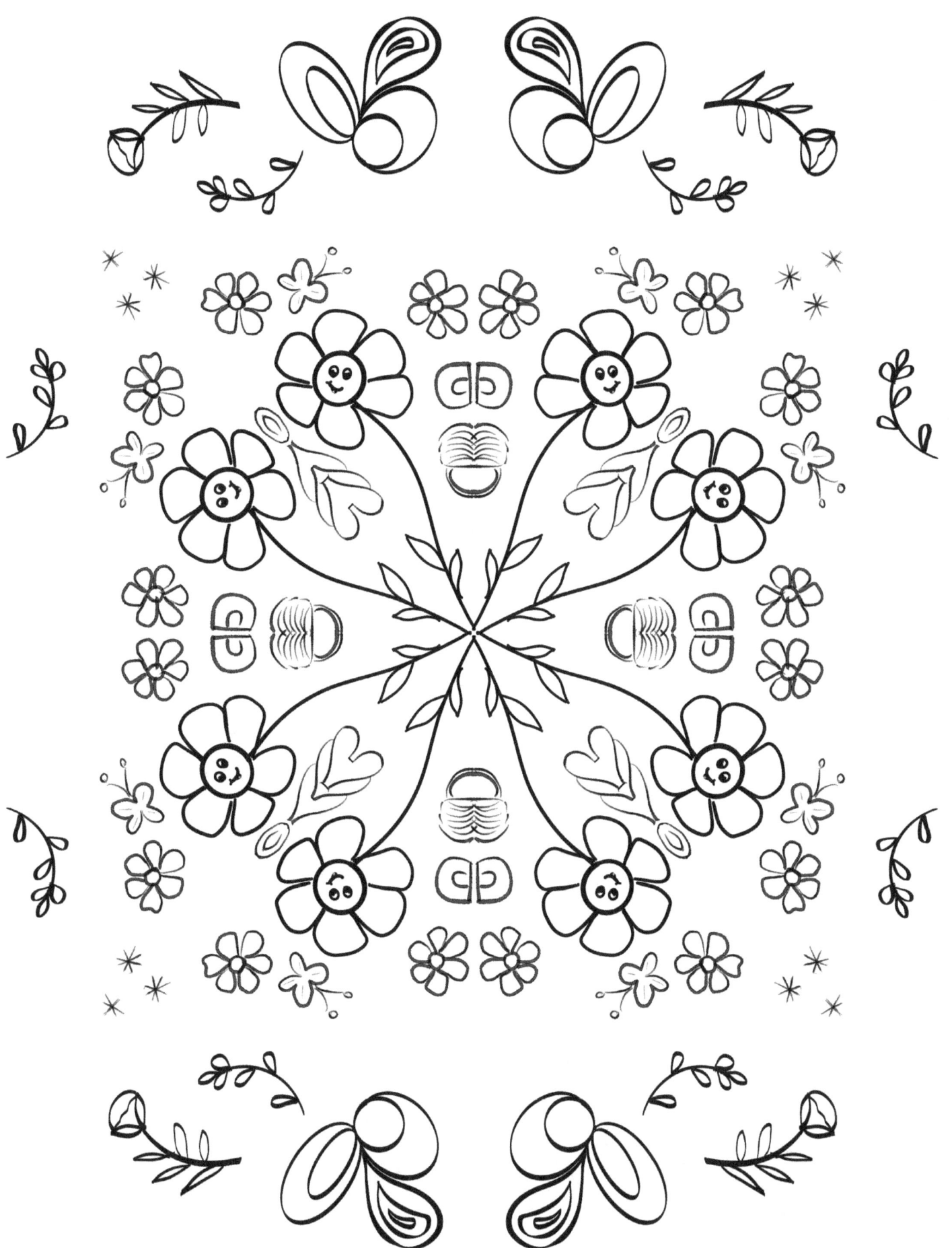

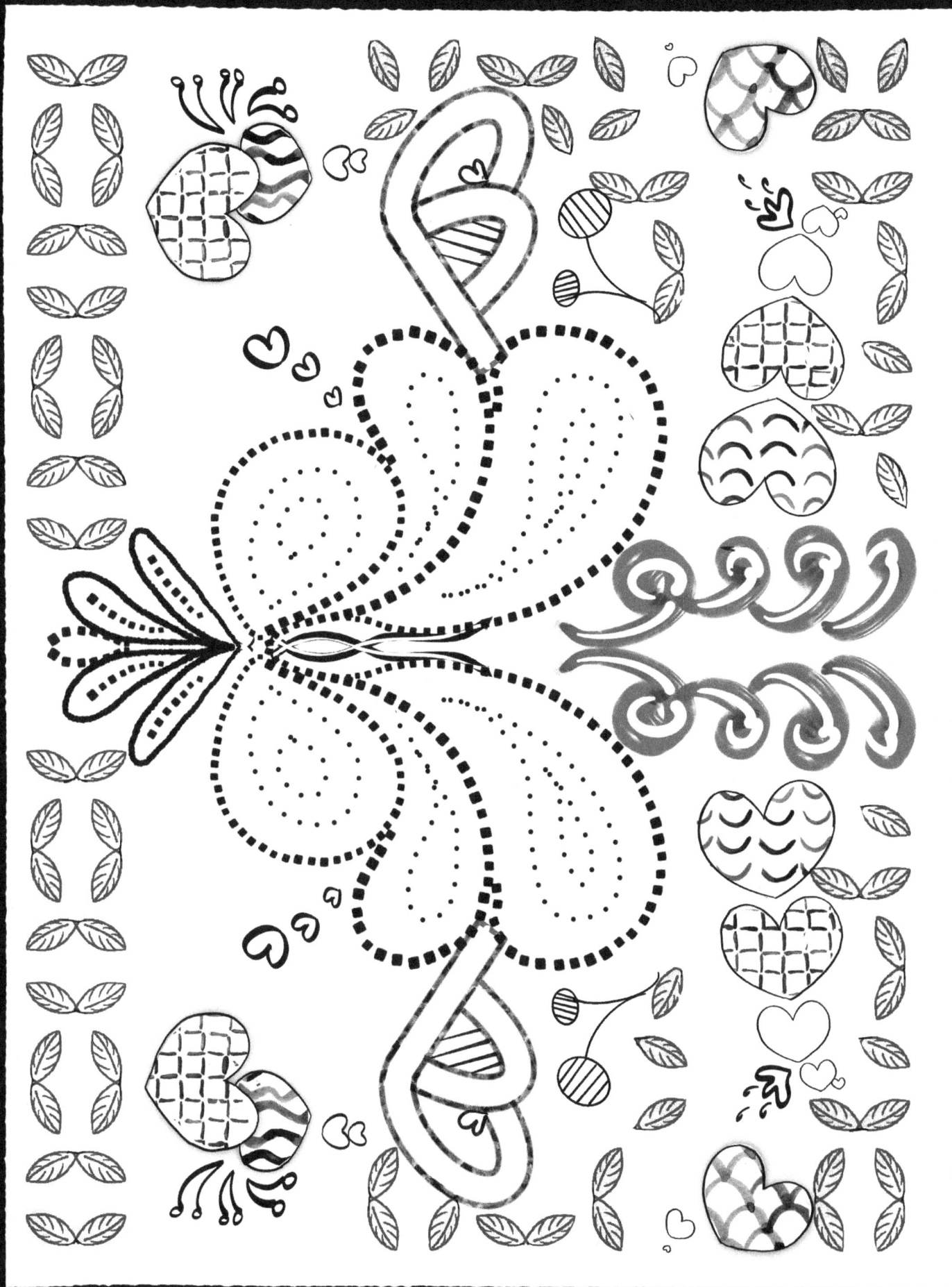

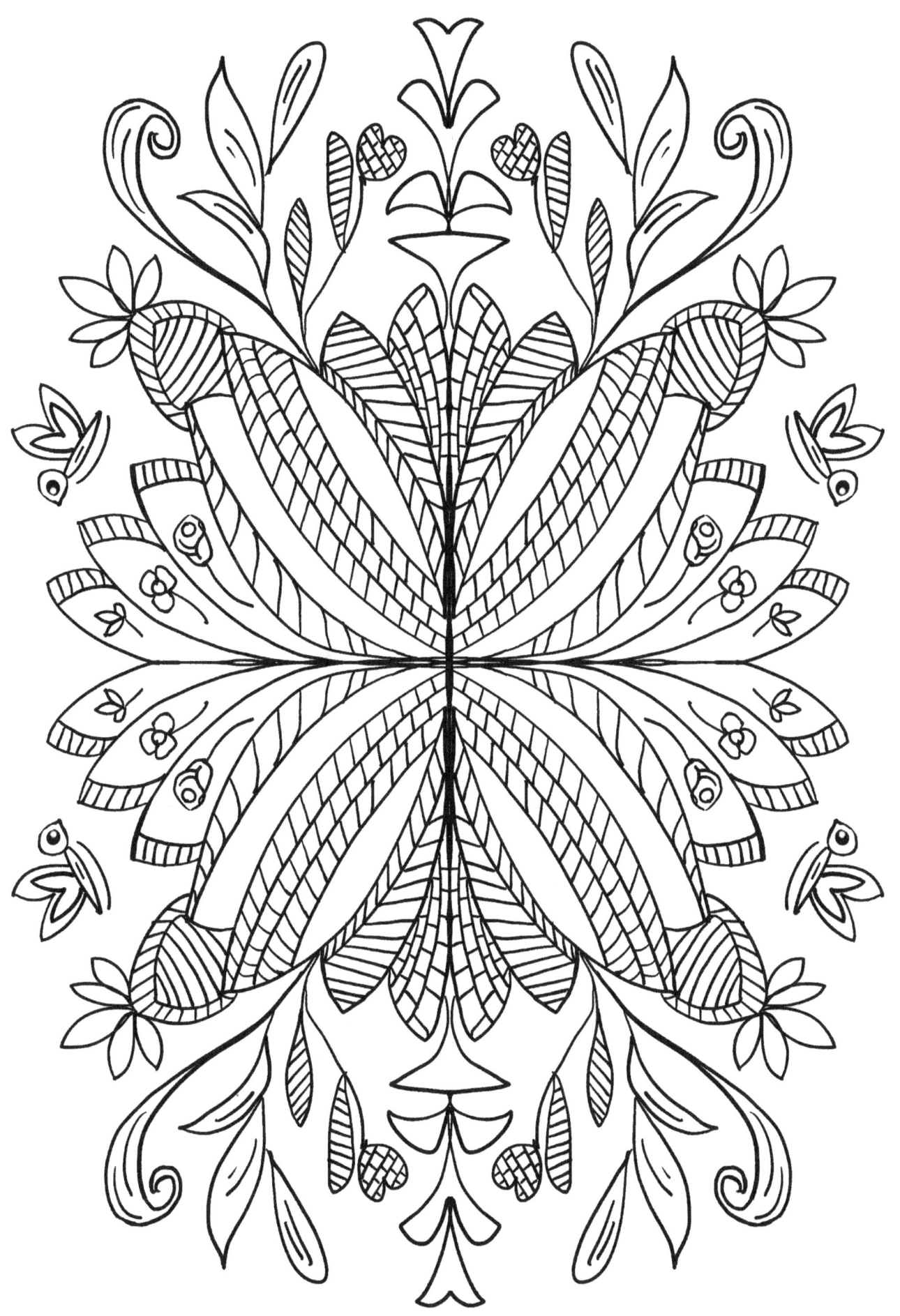

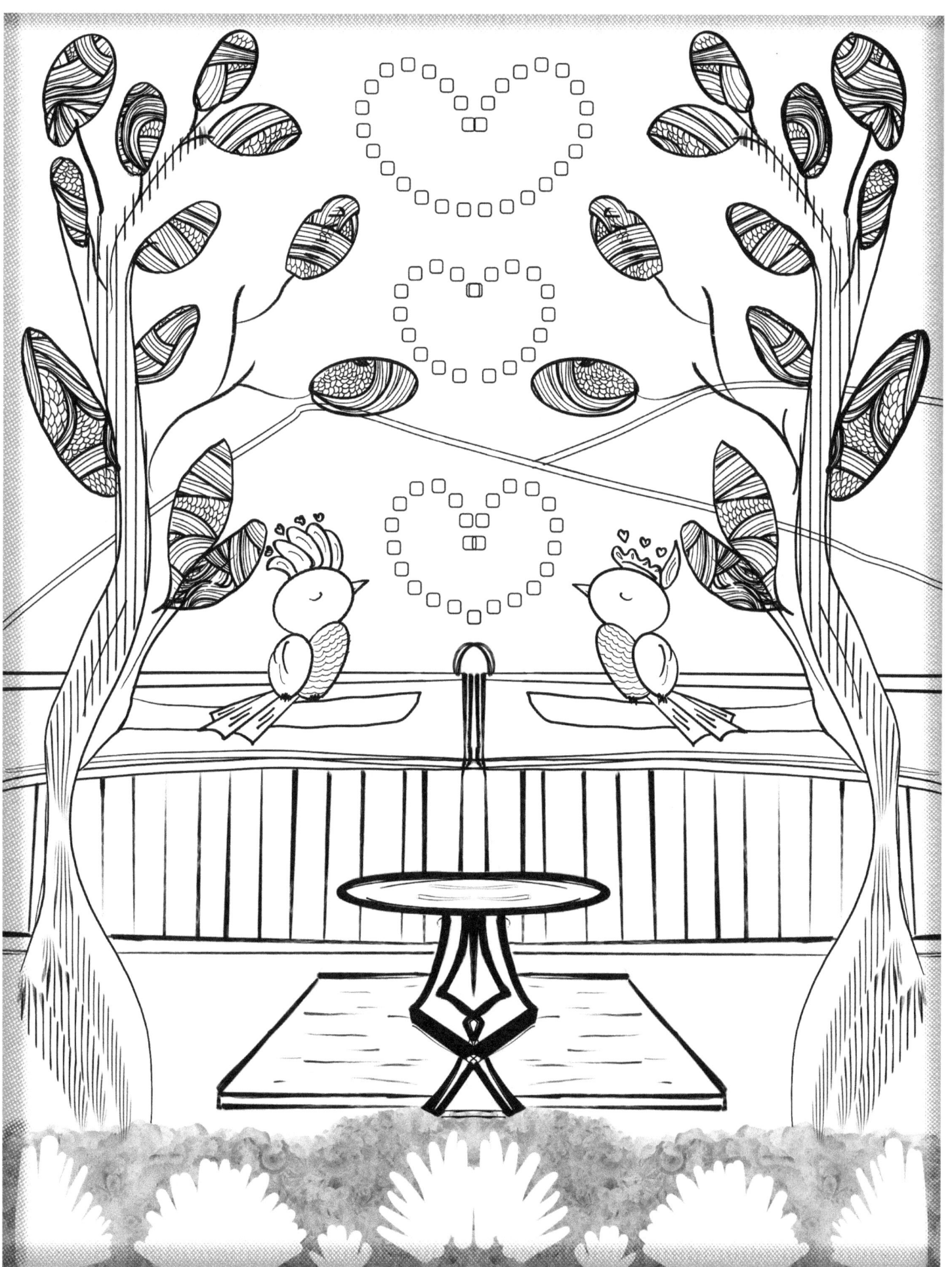

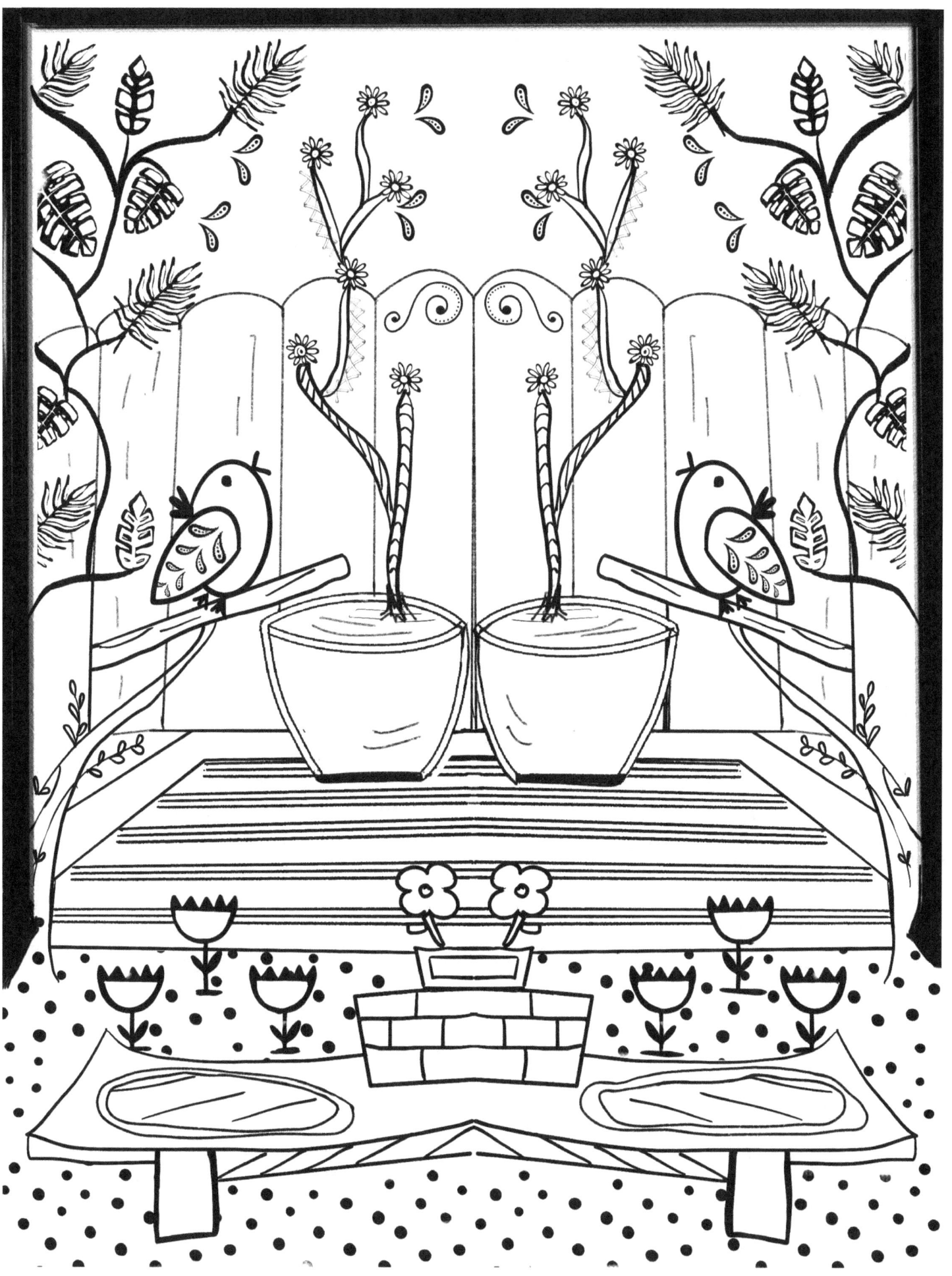

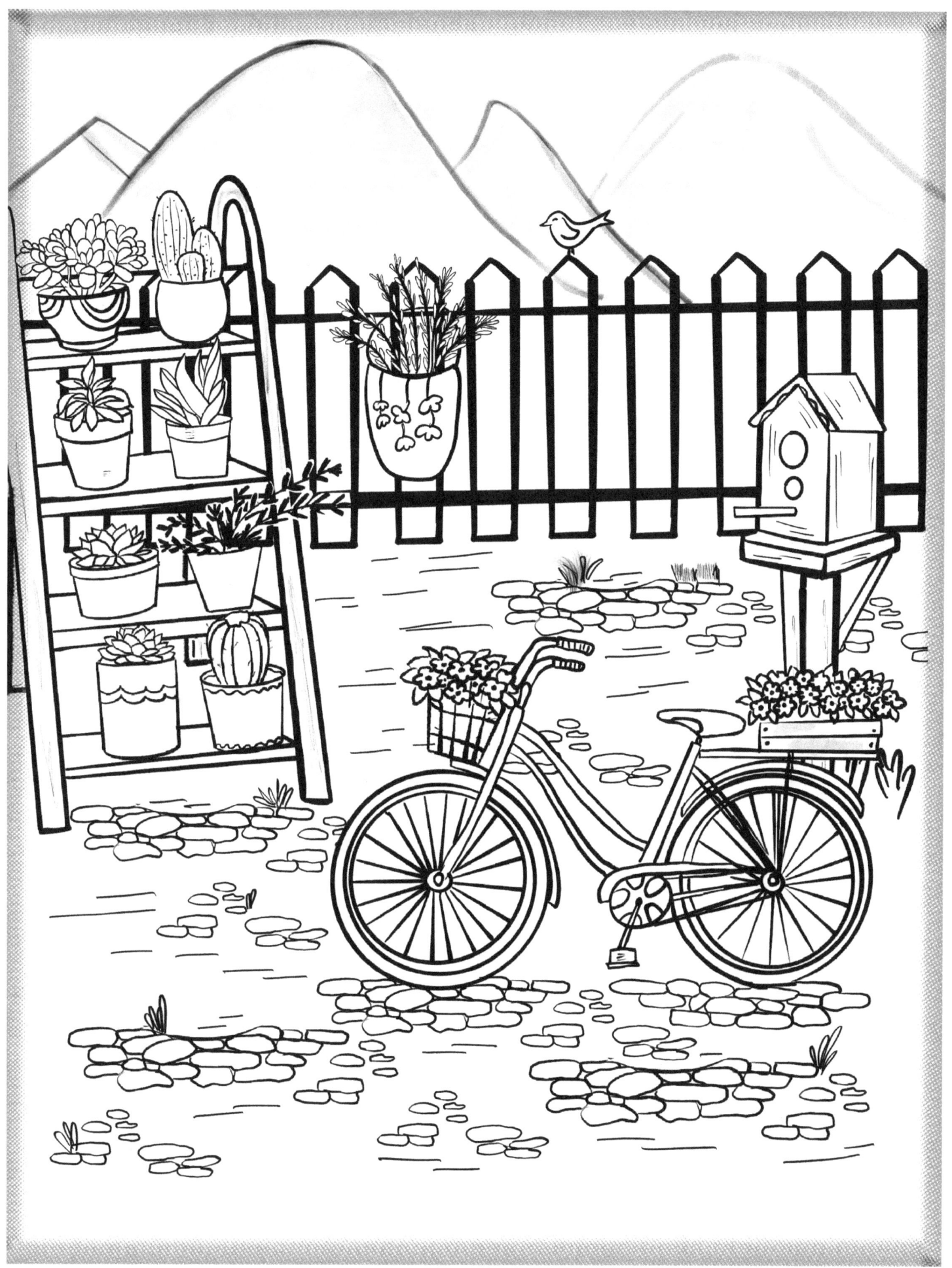

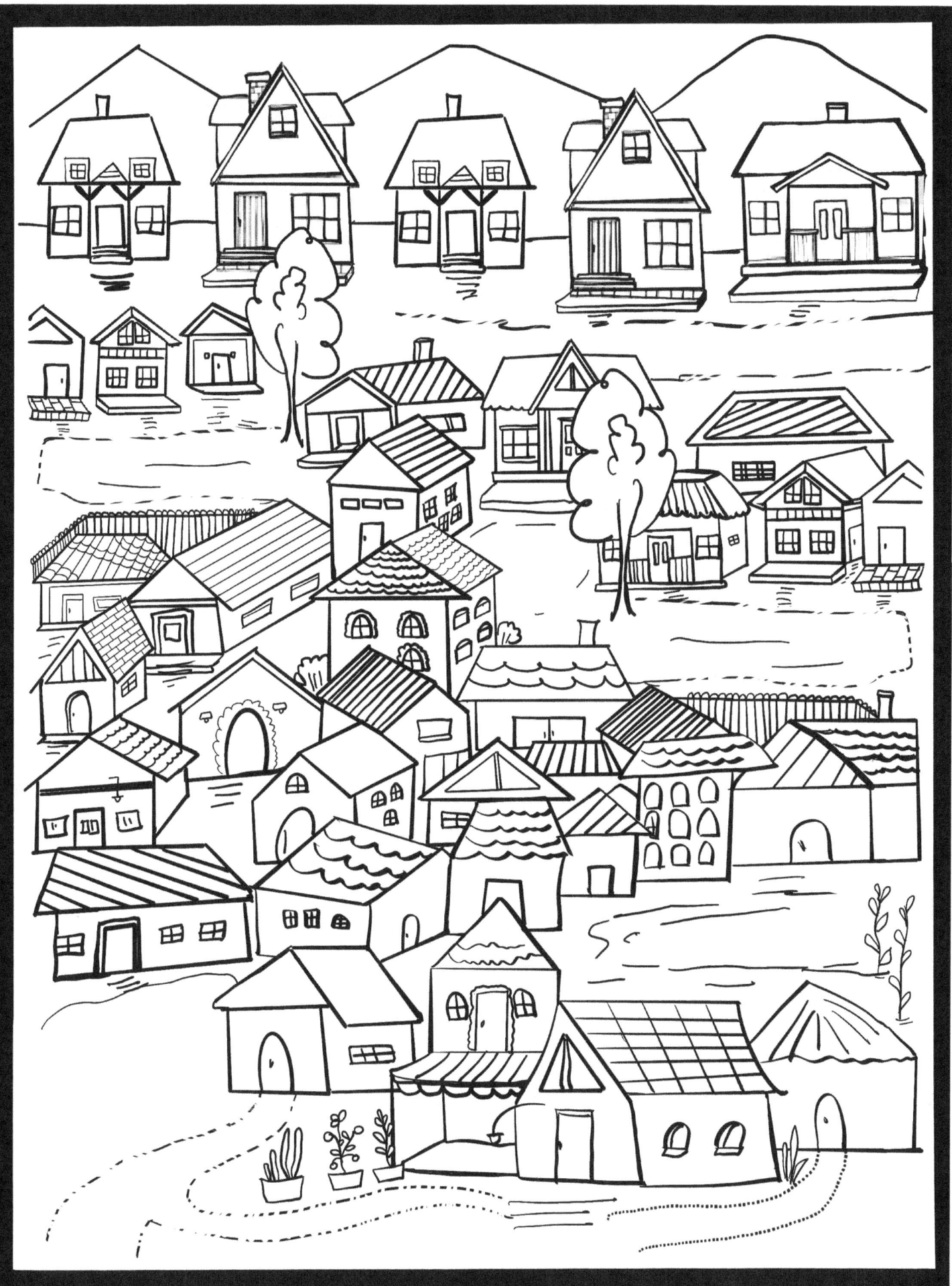

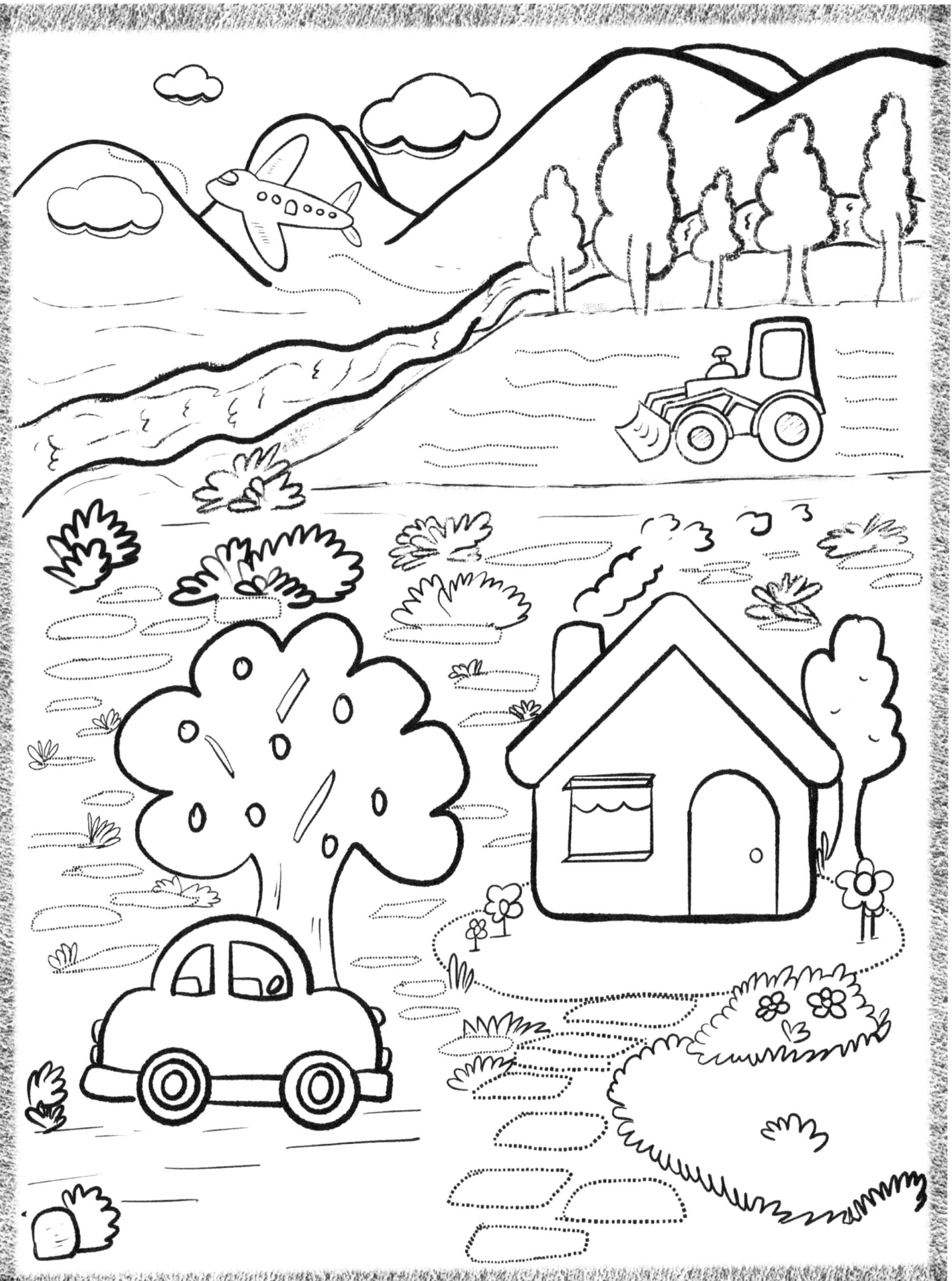

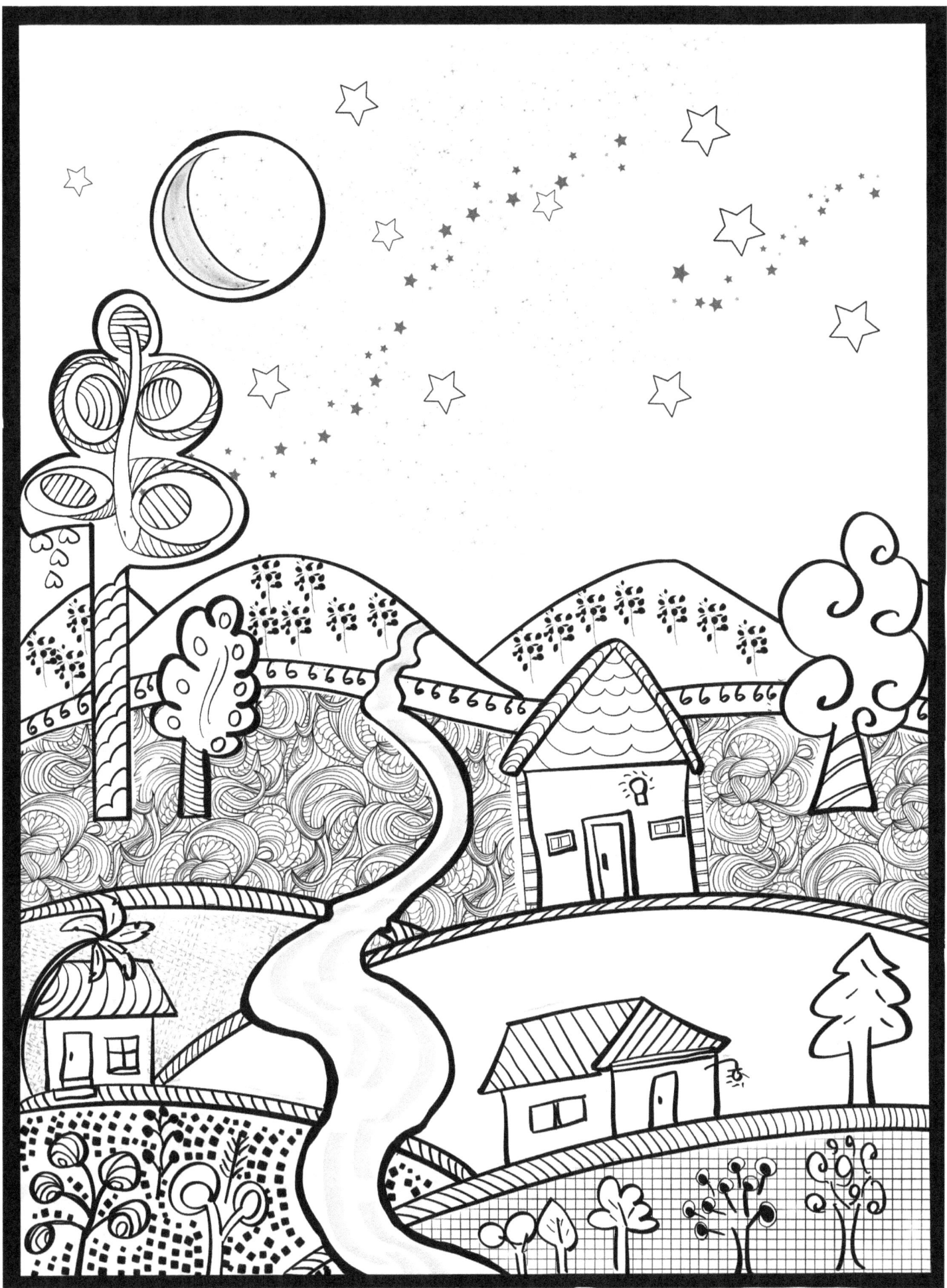

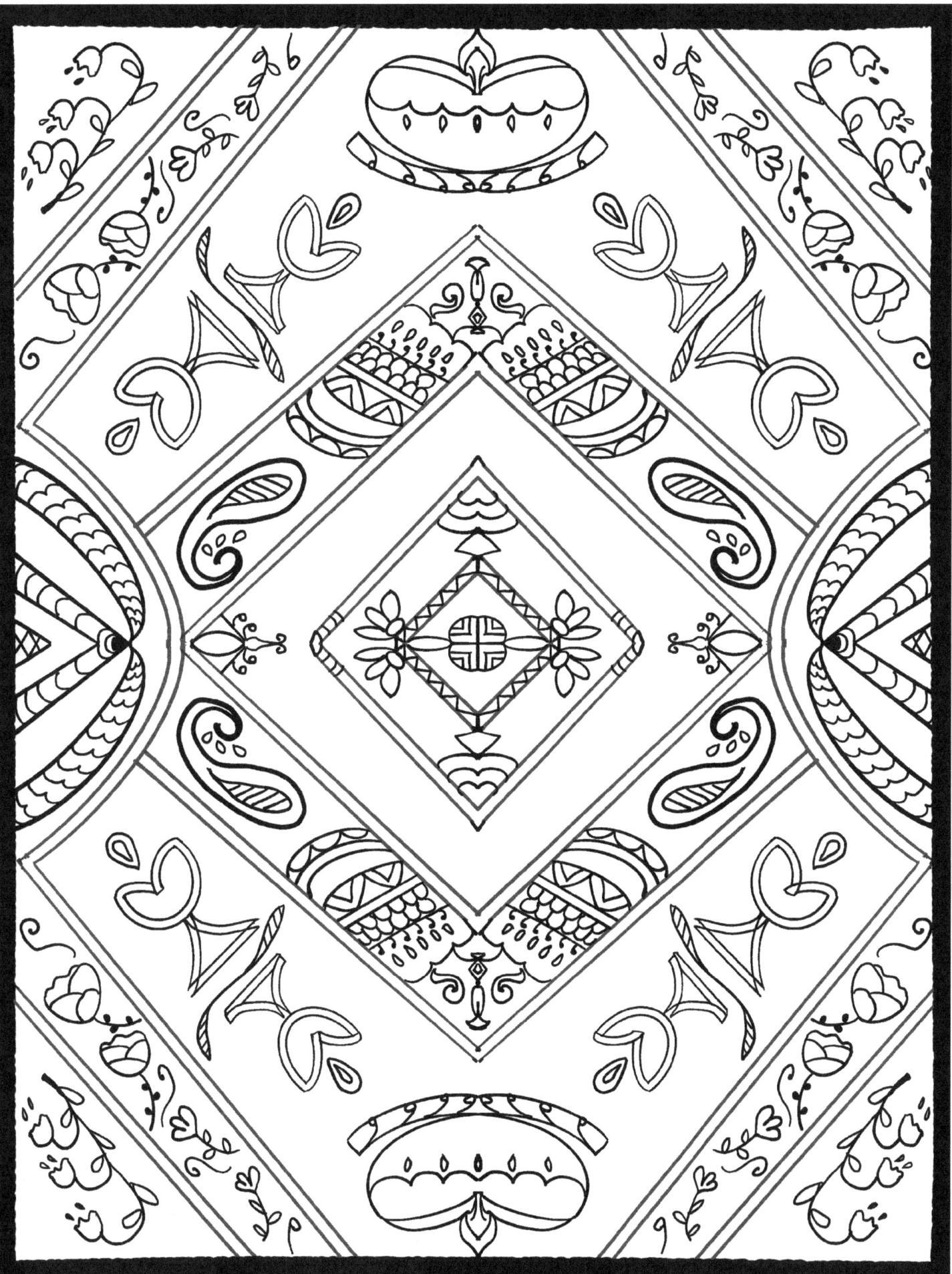

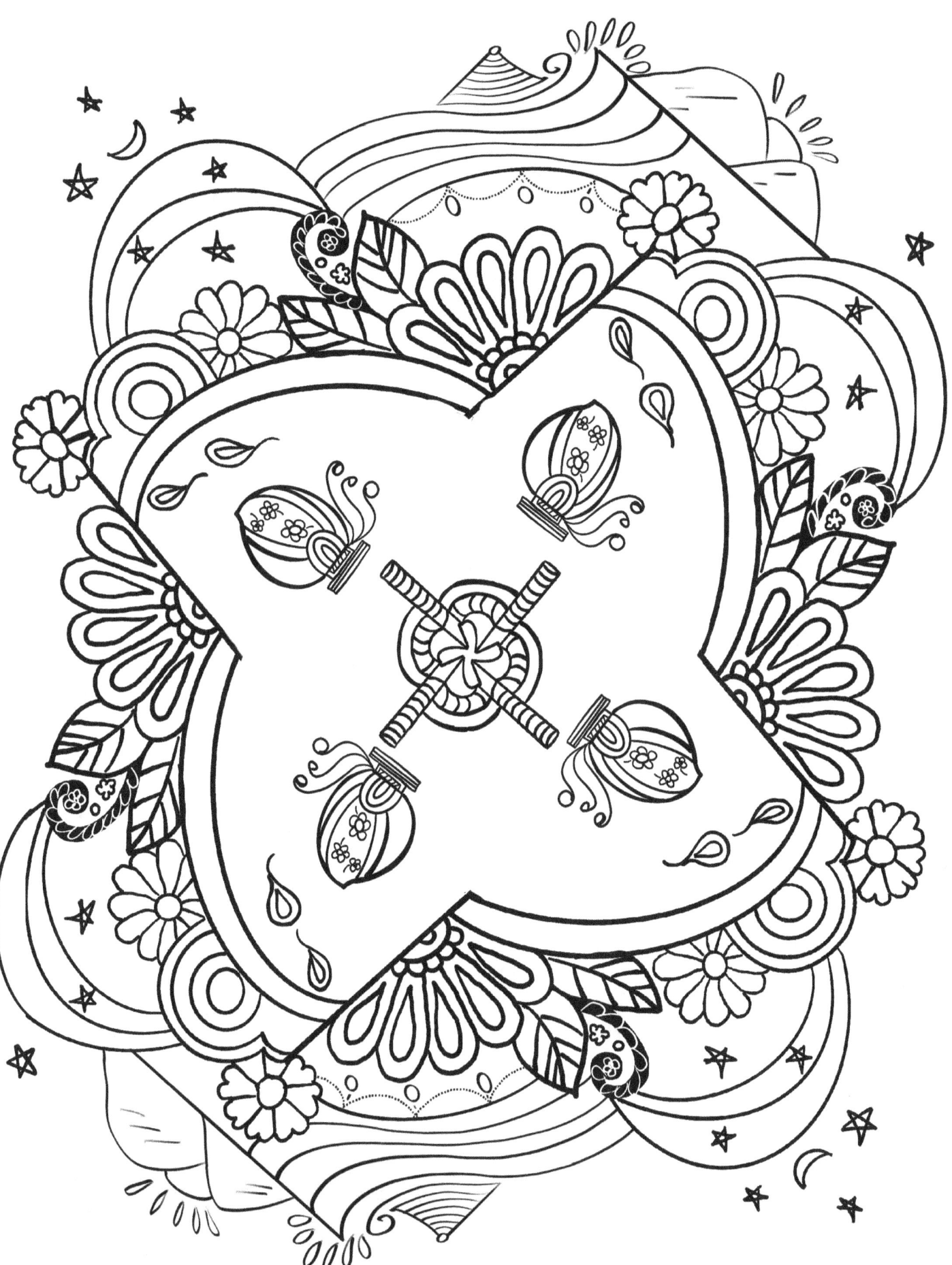

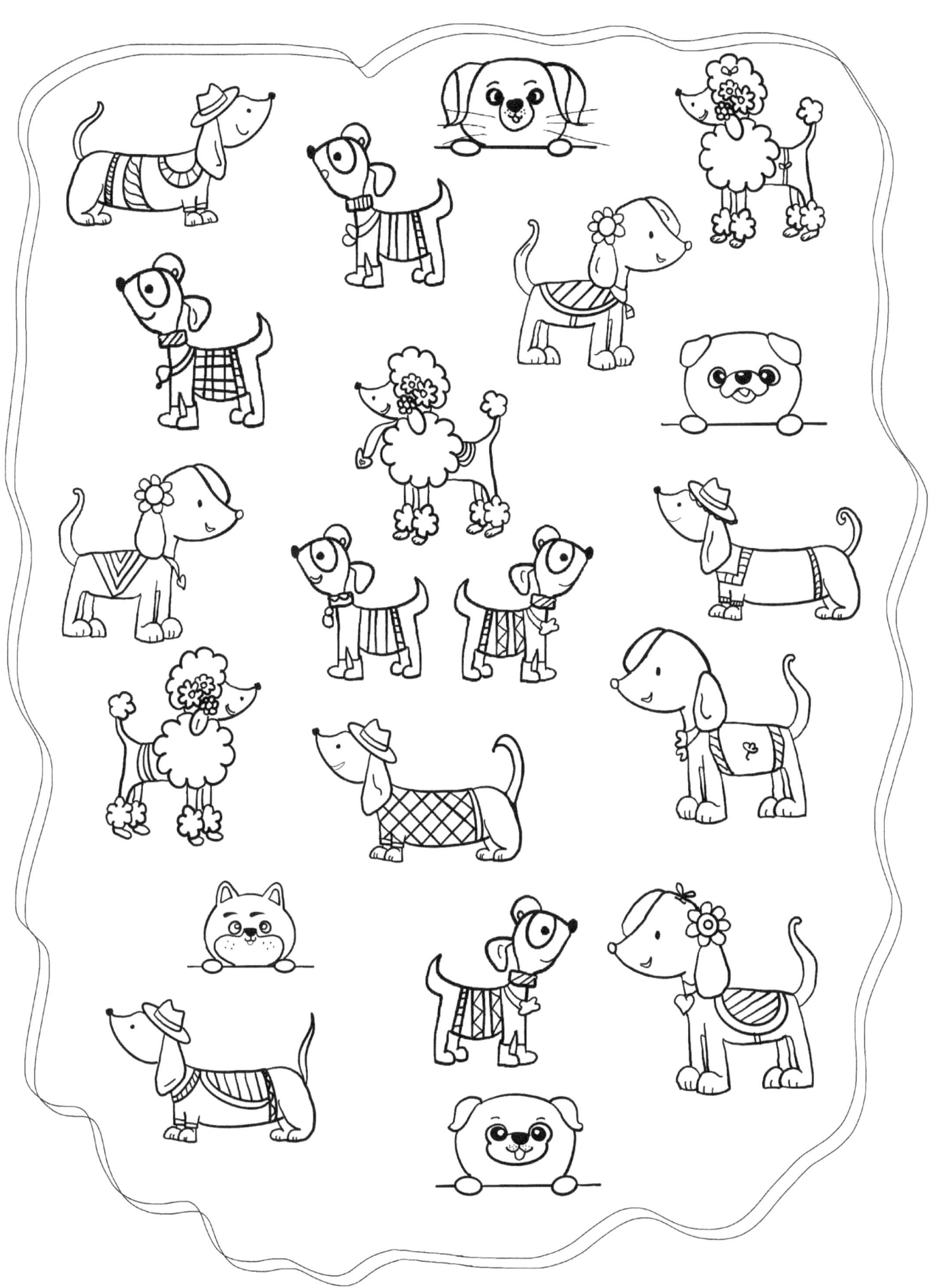

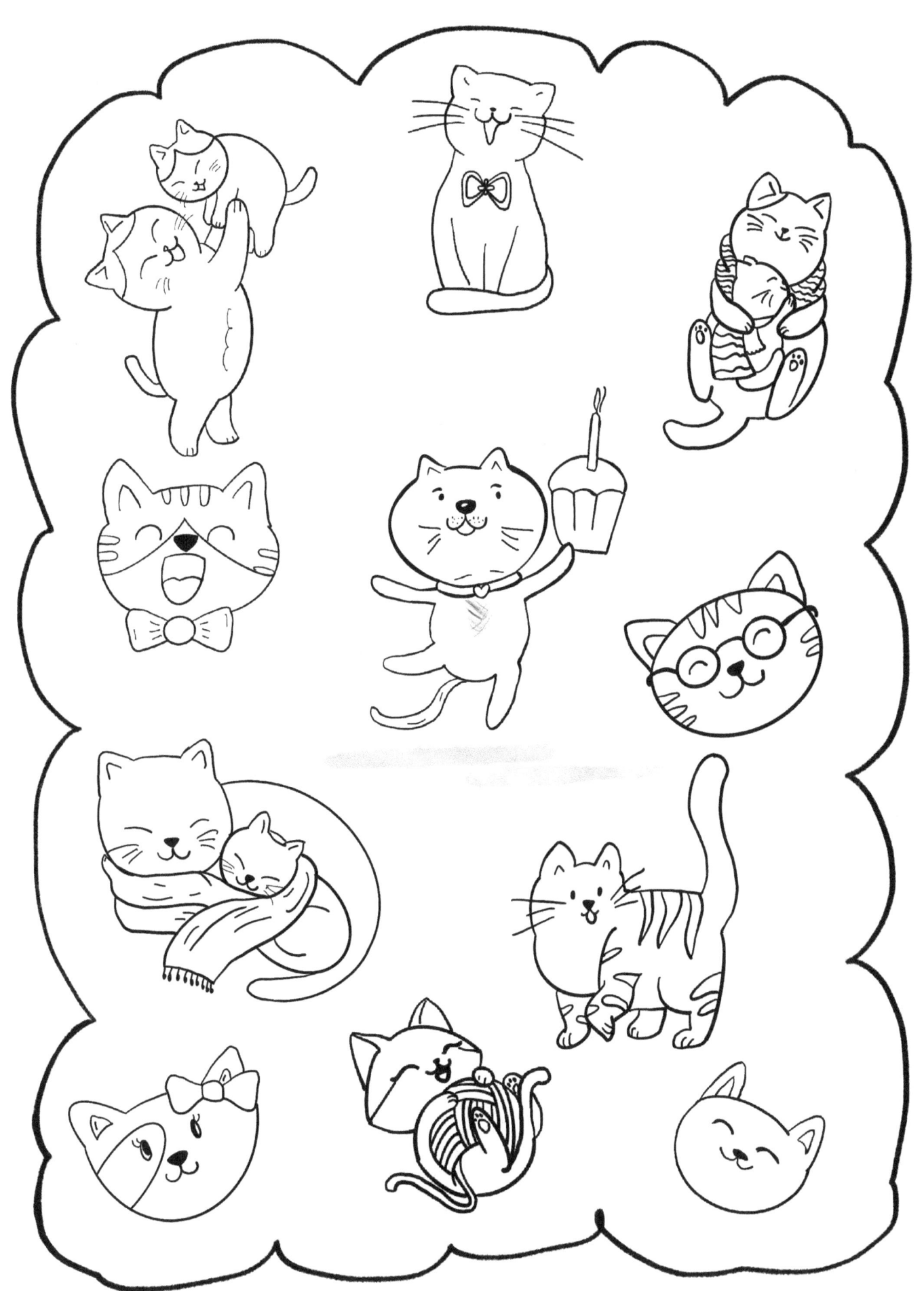

GUESS THE LANGUAGE

THANK YOU

MERCI

DANKE

GRACIAS

1. ENGLISH 2. FRENCH 3. GERMAN 4. SPANISH

GUESS THE LANGUAGE

xièxiè   谢谢

ARigatōgozaimasu
the 'u' is silent
ありがとうございました

DHANYAVAAD धन्यवाद

1. Chinese 2. Japanese 3. Hindi-Indian

Thank you for buying this book. I hope you enjoyed it and will share your colorful creations with me on my Facebook page or Instagram with the #

@Navitalovescolors

www.ingramcontent.com/pod-product-compliance
Lightning Source LLC
Chambersburg PA
CBHW081458220526
45466CB00008B/2698